My First Pony

KINGFISHER

Kingfisher Publications Plc,
New Penderel House,
283–288 High Holborn,
London WC1V 7HZ
www.kingfisherpub.com

First published by Kingfisher
Publications Plc 2005
10 9 8 7 6 5 4 3 2 1

1TR/0305/LFG/CLSN(CLSN)/140MA/F

ISBN-13: 978 0 7534 1101 8
ISBN-10: 0 7534 1101 6

A CIP catalogue record for this book
is available from the British Library.

Printed in China

Author: Judith Draper
Consultant: Elwyn Hartley Edwards
Editors: Jennifer Schofield, Russell Mclean
Designer: Poppy Jenkins
Photographer: Matthew Roberts
Hair and make-up: Isobel Bulat
Picture research manager: Cee Weston-Baker
Production manager: Nancy Roberts
DTP manager: Nicky Studdart
Proofreader and indexer: Sheila Clewley

Clothing and equipment supplied by
Dublin, Cuddly Ponies and Roma.

Ponies supplied and produced by
Justine Armstrong-Small BHSAI,
pictured with Zin Zan (Champion
Working Hunter and Supreme Horse,
Horse of the Year Show 2003;
Reserve Champion, Royal
International; Champion
Working Hunter, Horse
of the Year Show 2004).

My First Pony

Judith Draper

Contents

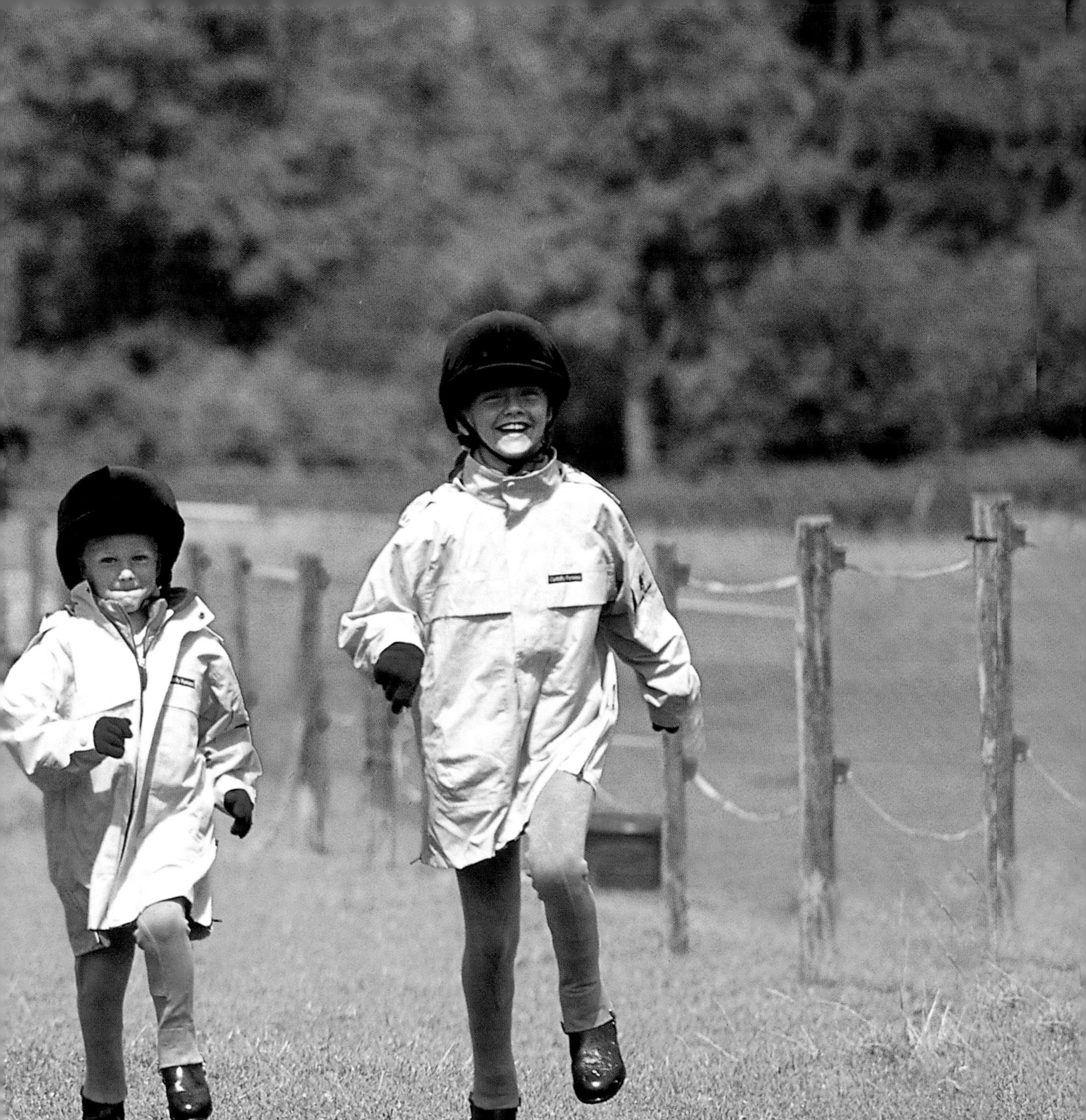

What is a pony?

A pony is a member of the horse family, which also includes asses and zebras. It is smaller than a horse, and has shorter legs. Ponies are many different sizes and colours, depending on which breed they belong to.

Horse

Pony

Measuring up

To find out how tall your pony is, measure him at the withers. These are the top of the pony's shoulders, between his neck and back. You can measure him in hands or centimetres.

On the withers
This sliding bar allows you to read off the pony's height. Rest it on the highest point of the withers.

Made to measure
This special pole is called a measuring stick. _____

No shoes
To find your pony's true height, stand him on level ground. He should not be wearing shoes.

Top tip

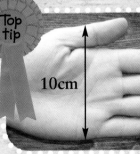

10cm

Hands
One hand equals about ten centimetres, which is roughly the width of an adult's hand.

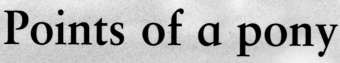

Points of a pony

Each part of a pony's body has its own special name. These are known as the 'points' of the pony. You will recognize some of the names, such as knee and elbow, because they describe parts of our bodies too.

Kind eyes

When you choose a pony, look for one with big eyes and a kind expression. This usually means that he is friendly.

croup

dock

hindquarters

back

tail

flanks

hindleg

belly

Hock

This joint works like your ankle. Ponies need strong hocks to carry the weight of a rider and to jump.

heel

Hoof and sole

A pony's foot has a hard covering called the hoof. The underneath of the foot is known as the sole.

8

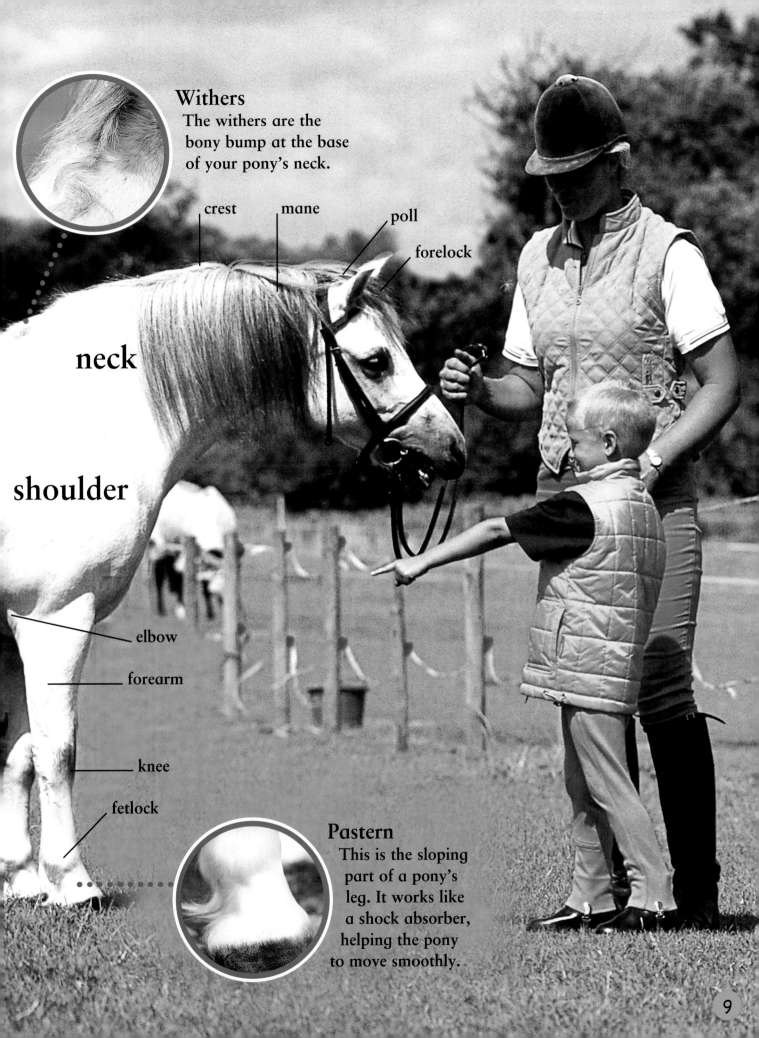

Withers
The withers are the bony bump at the base of your pony's neck.

crest

mane

poll

forelock

neck

shoulder

elbow

forearm

knee

fetlock

Pastern
This is the sloping part of a pony's leg. It works like a shock absorber, helping the pony to move smoothly.

Horse and pony breeds

There are more than 150 different breeds and types of horses and ponies. A breed is a horse or pony group that has been bred carefully over a period of time. A type is a horse or pony that is used for a particular job, such as a hunter or a riding pony.

Stock Horse
The tough and fast Australian Stock Horse is used for cattle herding. Until 200 years ago there were no horses in Australia, so the Stock Horse is a mixture of breeds from other countries.

Arab
The Arab is the oldest and purest of all horse breeds. It is small and strong, and moves with a beautiful 'floating' action. Arabs are high-spirited and playful, but gentle too.

Haflinger
This sturdy pony is named after a mountain village in Austria. It is sure-footed and makes a good riding or driving pony. All Haflingers are chestnut in colour.

Thoroughbred

This is the fastest breed of horse in the world, and makes a perfect racehorse. Thoroughbreds are strong, but they can be nervous and are not always easy to ride.

Quarter Horse

This American horse got its name because it used to be raced over a distance of a quarter of a mile (about 0.4 kilometres). It is very popular in Western riding.

Pony of the Americas

This pony was first bred in the USA in the 1950s. It has an eye-catching spotted coat, a kind nature, and makes a good riding pony.

Top tip

Welsh Pony

The beautiful Welsh Pony, or Section B, is probably the best riding pony in the world. It is perfect for shows and competitions.

Socks and stripes

Most horses and ponies have some white markings, either on their face or on their legs – and in many cases on both. Each marking has a special name, such as a sock or a stripe. These names are very useful for telling one pony from another.

Star and snip

Blaze

Stripe
A long, thin white mark down a pony's face is called a stripe.

Face marks

A wide white band down your pony's face is known as a blaze, while a thin band is a stripe. A white mark on a pony's forehead is a star. On the muzzle it is called a snip.

Colours

Most ponies are a shade of brown or grey, and have dark skin. Some grey ponies are born dark and become paler as they grow older. Each coat colour has a special name.

Dun

Skewbald

Chestnut

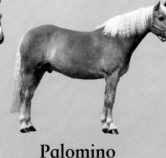

Palomino

Dark bay

Grey

Leg marks

If your pony has a white mark that reaches from his foot to above his knee, we say that he has a stocking. A shorter white mark is called a sock.

Bright bay

Sock
A white mark from the foot to just below the hock or knee is called a sock.

Top tip

Spotted coat
Some ponies are spotted. They have dark spots on a white coat, or white spots on a dark coat.

13

What to wear

Riding clothes are made to keep you safe and comfortable. The two most important things are a hard hat and safe boots. You can ride in jeans, but close-fitting jodhpurs are better because they stop your legs from being rubbed or pinched by the saddle.

Top tip

Neat hair
If you have long hair, make sure it is tied back, plaited or tucked into a hairnet for riding. Flapping hair looks untidy and gets in the way when you ride.

Riding hat
Your hat should fit you properly. Adjust the safety harness so that your hat does not slip in any direction.

Gloves
These help you to grip the reins. Gloves also stop your hands from becoming sore.

Jodhpurs
These have special patches on the insides of the knees to give you extra grip when you are riding.

Keep safe
Body protectors were first made for jockeys. They help to prevent injuries if you fall. You should definitely wear one when you are jumping.

Jodhpur boots
Always wear jodhpur boots. Never ride in trainers because they can easily get stuck in the stirrup irons.

Tack

A pony's saddle, bridle and any other equipment that he wears is known as tack. All tack must be kept clean and in good condition. Dirty and worn tack can make your pony sore.

cantle

stirrup iron

pommel

girth

stirrup leather

headpiece

browband

cheekpiece

noseband

numnah

bit

throatlash

reins

Saddle
The saddle must fit the pony perfectly. It must also be the right size for the rider.

Bridle
This is the headgear. It is made up of the headpiece and throatlash, the browband, cheekpieces, noseband, reins, and the 'bit' which fits in the pony's mouth.

Safety first!
Safety stirrups have an elastic side to stop your feet from being caught in the iron if you fall off.

Safety first!

Check your pony's paddock for dangerous objects, such as rusty wire, broken glass or bits of metal. If you find any, ask an adult to help you take them away.

Top tip

Plant alert

Many plants, such as ragwort, are poisonous to horses. Ask an adult to help you dig these up and burn them.

In the paddock

Ponies love to wander far and wide, eating grass. Nowadays a paddock is the nearest thing to a natural home that we can give them. It must have a trough of clean water, and a shelter to protect ponies from wet weather or the hot sun. Cows make good companions for ponies in a paddock.

No way out
The paddock must be surrounded by a strong fence to keep your pony from getting out. Wooden fencing is perfect for a pony paddock.

Electric fence
A paddock may be divided up by electric fencing. While your pony is grazing one part of the field, the grass in the other section has a chance to grow back.

Frisky pony
Keep a safe distance from a frisky pony when he is enjoying a canter round his field.

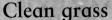

Warm rug
In the winter your pony may need to wear a waterproof rug in the paddock, to keep him warm, dry and comfortable.

Clean grass
Your pony's droppings may contain the eggs of worms that could make him ill. Clear away the droppings from the field regularly.

Top
tip

Kick bolt

Fit a kick bolt at
the bottom of the
door so that your
pony cannot get
out from his stable.

Ponies in stables

Being cooped up in a stable is very unnatural
for a pony, but it is sometimes necessary. Ponies
who are fit and competing are stabled because they
need to have a controlled diet. An injured or sick
pony may need to be kept stabled until he is better.
But stabled ponies should be allowed, whenever
possible, to spend part of each day in their paddock.

Mucking out

Keeping your pony's stable clean is a very important job. Wet bedding and droppings should be removed each morning and any droppings picked up regularly during the day.

Night rug

In cold weather ponies need a warm rug at night. This will stay in place even if the pony lies down and rolls.

Fresh water

Your pony's water bucket should be emptied regularly, cleaned, and refilled with fresh water.

Bedding

The stable floor needs a good covering of bedding to prevent your pony from hurting himself when he lies down. Straw, shredded paper, wood shavings and rubber matting are all suitable.

Food and water

Grass is a pony's natural food. But if you ride your pony regularly it will not give him enough energy. Also, in winter there is not enough goodness in the grass, even for a pony who is not working. This is why ponies need hay and other foods to keep them healthy.

Haynet
A haynet stops your pony from treading on the hay and wasting it.

Hanging high
Tie the haynet to a ring in the wall, high enough to stop your pony from catching his feet in it.

Water
Make sure that your pony always has a supply of clean water that he can reach easily.

Top tip

Quick release
Tie the haynet to the wall with a quick-release knot. This makes it easy to undo when the haynet is empty.

Short feed
Hay and grass are called bulk feed, and form the main part of a pony's diet. Other foods are known as short feeds. They are mixed together and fed in a bowl or manger.

Little and often

Ponies need to eat a lot of food, but only in small amounts. Otherwise they may become ill. Always feed your pony at the same times each day, and never ride him straight after feeding.

Tasty treat

Most ponies love carrots. Always cut them longways, not in rings or chunks, which could make your pony choke.

Feed bins

Keep all your pony's feed in clean, mouseproof containers, with lids that fit firmly. Plastic dustbins are perfect.

Some types of pony feeds

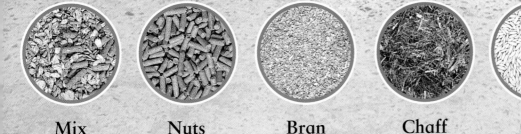

Mix   Nuts   Bran   Chaff   Oats   Barley

Worming

Make sure that your
pony is treated
regularly for worms.
You can give him
powder with his
food or squirt a
special paste into
his mouth. Ask an
adult to help you.

Happy and healthy

It is not difficult to tell if your pony is well.
A healthy pony has a shiny coat. He enjoys
galloping about the paddock with his friends
and is interested in what is going on around
him. A pony whose coat is dull and who stands
on his own, with his head down and not
wanting to eat, is probably feeling poorly.

Trotting up
If your pony cannot
walk properly, this is
known as being lame.
The vet will watch
your pony as you
walk and trot him.
This helps the vet
to tell which leg is
causing the problem.

What to look for

Press your pony's ribs with your finger. If he is the right weight, you will be able to feel the bones but not see them. Then check your pony's ears, eyes, coat and feet.

Alert ears

Pricked ears show that a pony is interested in what is going on around him.

Bright eyes

A healthy pony has bright eyes. Dull eyes usually mean that he is not feeling well.

Shiny coat

Your pony should have a smooth, glossy coat. If the hairs are standing up he may be cold or unwell.

Safety first!

If your pony starts lying down and getting up a lot, and begins to sweat, he may have an illness called colic. This can be caused by eating too much. Your pony must be seen by a vet straight away.

Neat feet

A pony's hooves should be trimmed regularly to stop them cracking or growing too long.

23

Don't run

Ponies are easily startled by sudden movements or noises, so never run up to them or approach them from behind.

Lead on

There are times when you will need to use a headcollar to lead your pony – when you fetch him from his field, for example. When you go to catch him, make sure that he can see and hear you coming. Walk up to him calmly, speaking to him in a quiet voice.

Safety first!

Keep at a safe distance when you are walking with a pony who is being led. If he is feeling frisky, he may kick out.

On the left

When you lead a pony, walk on his left-hand side. This is his near side. Walk at your pony's shoulder, not in front of him.

Safe shoes

When you are near a pony, wear strong shoes or boots, not trainers, in case he steps on your foot by accident.

Lead rope

Hold the lead rope with both hands. The end must not trail on the ground, as it could trip you up. Never wrap the rope around your hand.

Putting on the headcollar

1 Stand on your pony's left side. Put the rope around his neck, slide on the noseband and take hold of the buckle

2 Fasten the headpiece on the left side. Make sure that you pass the loose end neatly through the buckle.

3 Check that the headcollar fits correctly – the noseband should lie well up the pony's nose, not low over his nostrils.

Clean and smart

Grooming means using different tools to brush your pony's coat, pick out his feet and clean his eyes, nose and around the top of his tail. Grooming helps to keep a pony healthy. It also makes him look smart and keeps his tack and your clothes clean.

Plastic or rubber curry comb
This is useful for removing dried mud and loose hairs.

Kit box
A special kit box is useful for keeping all your grooming tools together. When you are grooming, place it well away from your pony.

Top tip

Shiny coat
Use a cloth, called a stable rubber, to give your pony's coat a final shine after he has been groomed.

Dandy brush
This stiff brush is good for removing dried mud, but you must use it gently.

Body brush
This soft brush is used to groom the whole of the pony, including his head, mane and tail.

Metal curry comb
Use the metal curry comb to clean the body brush. Never use it on your pony.

Sponge
Use a damp sponge to wipe around a pony's eyes, and a different one to clean his nose.

Hoof pick
Before you go riding, always use a hoof pick to clean your pony's feet.

Hoof oil
On smart occasions, brush this oil on to your pony's feet to make them shine.

Safety first!
Never kneel or sit down on the floor when you groom your pony. Bend or squat down so that you can get out of the way quickly if he makes a sudden movement.

27

Tacking up

Knowing how to put on your pony's saddle and bridle – or 'tacking up' – is an important part of learning to ride. Always be gentle, never bang the saddle on to your pony's back, and take care not to hurt his eyes or ears.

Putting on the bridle

1 Put the reins over the pony's neck. Move your right arm under his jaw and hold the bridle. With your left hand, press the bit into his mouth.

2 Carefully pass the headpiece over the pony's ears. Pull his forelock over the browband.

3 Fasten the throatlash, but not too tightly. You should be able to fit the full width of your hand between it and the side of the pony's jawbone.

4 When the noseband is fastened, you should be able to slide two fingers between it and the pony's nose.

Putting on the saddle

1 Slide the saddle on to your pony's back from his left side. Make sure that the stirrup irons are at the top of the leathers and the girth is folded over the saddle.

2 Move round the pony and lower the girth, making sure it is not twisted. Go back to the left side and fasten the girth – not too tightly at first.

3 Use your hand to smooth out any wrinkles in the pony's skin and to check that the girth is tight enough.

Top tip

Saddle soap

To keep the tack clean and soft, sponge off all the dirt and grease, then rub special saddle soap into the leather.

First lesson

Riding lessons take place in an area called the school. In your first riding lesson you will learn how to get on and off your pony, and how to hold the reins. Mounting and dismounting may seem difficult at first, but they become much easier with practice.

Hands ahead
Your hands should be either side of the pony's neck, pointing straight ahead.

Mounting

1 Stand beside your pony, holding the reins and the front of the saddle in your left hand. Take the stirrup in your right hand and put your left foot in it.

2 Grip the far side of the saddle with your right hand. Spring up, straighten both legs and point your left toe down so that it does not dig into the pony's side.

3 Swing your right leg over the pony's back and let go of the saddle. Sit down gently in the saddle and put your right foot in the stirrup iron.

Positions please

Sit up tall in the deepest part of the saddle. To help you keep a good position, imagine a line running from the top of your head, through your elbows and hips to your heels. Keep your head up and look to the front.

Dismounting

1 Hold the reins in your left hand. Take both feet out of the stirrups and lean forwards slightly.

2 Swing your right leg up and over the saddle. Be careful not to kick your pony's back.

3 Hold the front of the saddle and slide down gently to the ground. Bend your knees as you land on your toes.

In the stirrups
Rest the ball of your foot on the stirrup iron. Your heel should be lower than your toes.

Top tip

Tight girth
To tighten the girth when mounted, hold the reins in your right hand, lift your leg and raise the saddle flap with your left hand.

Warming up

Mounted exercises are great fun and they help to make you supple. You will find it easier to ride if you do stretching exercises to warm up your muscles. Exercises also help to improve your balance, which will give you confidence. The best time to do them is before a lesson.

Zip up
Always zip up your body warmer before you start exercising. Loose clothes can get caught on the saddle.

Toe touch
You can do lots of fun stretching exercises on a pony. Try raising your right arm above your head, then stretch down to touch your left toe. Sit up straight and do it again, but this time touch your right toe with your left hand.

Safety first!
When you do a mounted exercise, your teacher should hold the pony to make sure that he does not move.

Round the world

This exercise looks difficult at first, but it is fun to do and is very good for your balance.

1 Begin by letting go of the reins and taking both feet out of the stirrups.

2 Hold on to the saddle and swing your right leg over the pony's neck to face sideways.

3 Swing your left leg over his back so that you are facing his tail. Be careful not to kick him.

4 Swing your right leg over so that you face the other side. Do not forget to move your hands.

5 Lastly, swing your left leg over his neck. Now you are back where you began, facing forwards.

On the move

To ask your pony to move forwards, turn corners and stop, you have to use signals called 'aids'. If at first your pony does not do what you want, it may be because you are not giving him the correct signals.

Walk on

Before you move off, you should be sitting up straight. To ask your pony to go from halt to walk, press his sides with your lower legs and say 'walk on'.

Halt

To stop, press the pony's sides with your legs and bring your hands back towards your body. When the pony stops, relax your hold on the reins.

Take a turn

Once you know how to ask your pony to move forwards and to stop, you can learn how to make turns. Remember to practise turning both left and right.

Right hand
To turn left, move your right hand forwards.

Left hand
At the same time, move your left hand outwards.

Top tip

Look first
Always look in the direction you want to turn, and keep your head up.

Turning left
To turn left, press your right leg against the pony's side behind the girth. Move your right hand forwards so that the pony can bend his head to the left. At the same time, move your left hand outwards. If you want to turn right, make the opposite movements.

Bouncy ride

To ask your pony to go from walk to trot, squeeze him with your lower legs. The trot feels less bumpy if you rise out of the saddle in time with the pony's strides. This is called the rising trot.

Sit down

Lower yourself gently into the saddle as the pony's outside foreleg hits the ground.

outside foreleg

Trot

The trot is a faster pace than walk. When your pony trots, his feet hit the ground two at a time, in diagonal pairs. This is quite different from walking, when he moves his legs one at a time. Trot is the most difficult pace for the rider to learn because it feels very bumpy at first.

Safety first!

Fit a neck strap on your pony. If you start to lose your balance, hold on to the neck strap or your pony's mane.

Rise up

Lift yourself slightly out of the saddle as the pony's inside foreleg touches the ground.

inside foreleg

Up and down

When you rise to the trot in a school, your weight should be in the saddle when the pony's outside foreleg (the leg nearest the fence) strikes the ground. Lift your weight out of the saddle as his inside foreleg (the leg nearest the centre of the school) touches the floor.

Top tip

One-two

When you are first learning to trot, call out 'up-down' or 'one-two' in time with your pony's strides.

Right leg first

To canter with the pony's right leg leading, keep your right leg on the girth and squeeze behind the girth with your left leg.

Leading leg

When he is cantering, the pony 'leads' with his left front leg if he is circling to the left. If he is circling to the right, he leads with his right front leg.

Canter

The canter is a faster pace than the trot. It is a very comfortable pace for the rider, but you may find it a little bumpy to begin with. To enjoy cantering you must learn to relax and stay sitting in the saddle.

Top tip

Practise!

Before you try to canter, practise the leg positions at halt. Move your left leg behind the girth to ask the pony to lead with his right leg.

Moving hands

Keep a light contact with your pony's mouth through the reins, but let your hands follow the movement of his head and neck.

Relax

In order to stay sitting down in the saddle, you must relax. This will help you to follow the pony's movements.

leading leg

Gallop

Ponies find it very exciting to gallop, which is the fastest pace of all. You should sit forwards, slightly out of the saddle. Let the pony stretch his neck, but do not lose contact with his mouth.

Safety first!

Never gallop until you can control your pony at walk, trot and canter. If you gallop with other riders, leave plenty of room between each pony.

Trotting over poles

Before your first jump, walk or trot over poles on the ground. It helps you and your pony get used to the rhythm of jumping.

look forwards

do not pull on the reins to keep your balance

Crossed poles

Always use a fence with crossed poles when you are learning to jump. Crossed poles help your pony to keep a straight line and to jump in the middle of the fence.

First jump

Jumping is one of the most exciting things that you can do with your pony, but it takes practice. You should not try to jump until you have learned to walk, trot and canter, and can ride turns and circles.

In position

You can practise the correct jumping position at halt. Your lower leg should be directly under you, not swinging back or pushed forwards. Remember to shorten your stirrup leathers by one or two holes when you are jumping.

Jumping a fence

1 As your pony approaches the fence, lean forwards into the jumping position. You should be sitting slightly out of the saddle.

2 At the fence, the pony pushes up with his hindquarters. Follow his movement, but do not throw yourself forwards. Do not drop the reins.

3 As you clear the fence, keep hold of the reins but allow the pony to stretch his head and neck. Try not to bump down into the saddle.

4 The last stage of a jump is called the get-away. You should be slightly out of the saddle as your pony moves away from the fence.

Western riding

Western riding is based on the easy-going style of the North American cowboys. They were often on horseback all day long, driving cattle over long distances. Horses that are ridden Western-style today are still taught many of the traditional movements that cowboys used.

Headstall
A loop that fits round one ear is called a split-ear headstall.

On the move
Sit in the deepest part of the saddle with a long stirrup, so that your legs are nearly straight. Hold the reins loosely and keep your hands high.

Walk
Click with your tongue and squeeze lightly with your legs to move from halt to walk.

Jog
Use the same signals to go into jog, which is the Western horse's slow, relaxed trot.

Lope
Squeeze with your outside leg to ask your horse to go into the lope, which is a steady canter.

cheekpiece

crownpiece

Bit
The Western bit has long sidepieces called shanks. Use the bit very gently, otherwise you can hurt your horse's mouth.

Horn
Cowboys tied a rope to the horn when they were catching cattle.

What to wear
For everyday Western riding, you can wear easy-fitting casual clothes, such as a pair of jeans and a shirt, with jodhpur boots or cowboy boots.

Top tip

Dismount
Hold the horn with your right hand, swing your right leg over and place your foot on the ground. Then take your left foot out of the stirrup.

cantle

back jockey

skirt

seat jockey

fender

tie strap

cinch

Stirrups
Western stirrups are made of wood or plastic, and are often covered with leather.

Hacking out

Going for a ride in the countryside, or hacking, is great fun. Ponies like to see new places too! You can explore woods and commons, or canter along a bridleway with your friends.

Bright lights

To make sure that motorists can see you, always wear light-reflecting safety gear, such as a belt and a hat band.

All together

Until you are older, you should always go hacking with an adult.

Gates

To prevent farm animals from getting out of their field, always close any gates you go through. With practice, you can open and close gates without dismounting.

Top tip

Be alert

Enjoy your hack, but remember to ride properly and to stay alert in case you meet something unfamiliar that might startle your pony.

Fun and games

Competitions are fun. There are many kinds of games and races for you and your pony to try. Some are for teams, but there are also competitions that you can take part in on your own.

Gymkhana games

A competition with races and mounted games is called a gymkhana. If your pony is small and quick, he will be good at races such as bending, where you weave in and out of a line of cones.

Get dressed
You can wear your smartest clothes for a gymkhana, or something more casual, such as a sweatshirt.

Dressage
In a dressage test, you ride at walk, trot and canter, and do turns and circles in a particular order. Your pony must be very well trained and obedient. Both of you should look extra neat and tidy.

Bending race

Show jumping

In show jumping, you have to ride over a course of coloured fences, trying not to knock any of them down.

Hunter trials

Cross-country jumping competitions are called hunter trials. The course is laid out across fields. Unlike in show jumping, the fences do not fall down if you hit them.

Safety first!

Before you ride in a hunter trial, walk round the course so that you can work out the best way to jump each fence.

Top tip

Show-smart

Always groom your pony, clean your tack and polish your boots before a show or competition, so that you both look super-smart.

Index

Acknowledgements

The publisher would like to thank the following for their help in the production of this book:

Models: Charley, Ellie, Elliot, Fraser, Hollie, Nirvana and Rhianna

Ponies: Chip, Jasper, Pickwick, Piglet, Pikie, Prince, Silver and Teddy

The Justine Armstrong-Small team (www.armstrong-small.co.uk): Justine and Hazel Armstrong-Small Grooms: Amy, Becky, Katie, Keeley, Lisa, Rosie and Vicky

Dublin, Cuddly Ponies and Roma (www.weatherbeeta.com)

Photography: Matthew Roberts (www.matthewrobertsphotographer.com)

David and Sarah Deptford (www.sovereignquarterhorses.com)

The Ada Cole Rescue Stables (www.adacole.co.uk)

All at Bumbles Green Farm

All photographs by Matthew Roberts with the exception of: page 10cl, 10tr, 11tr, 11cr, 13br, 16bl, 27tr, 45bl, 47tl (Bob Langrish, www.boblangrish.co.uk)